Want to Know
nature

The Rabbit

Written by Jozua Douglas
Illustrated by Hiky Helmantel

Clavis
NEW YORK

It's Grandpa's birthday. Brad got him a nice present. It's a big box with holes in it. Quickly, Grandpa opens it. "A rabbit!" he exclaims. "I love it! What a great addition to the family."

What's a rabbit?

A tame rabbit loves to be held and cuddled. Rabbits usually live to be seven or eight years old.

Most rabbits have big, long **ears**. That's why they can hear extremely well. Can you hear the cat sneak through the grass? Can you hear the fox in its den? The rabbit hears everything. It moves its long ears in all directions. It knows the location of each noise.

Did you know
the biggest rabbit on earth measures more than three feet long? That's almost your length!

The rabbit's **eyes** are on the side of its head. That way, it can see what's happening next to it and even behind it. Rabbits see the world differently than you do. They can see far and detect moving objects. And just like a cat, they can see extremely well in the dark and at dusk.

Thanks to its **whiskers**, a rabbit can easily sense its surroundings. This is useful when it crawls through dark tunnels. Rabbits also have responsive nerve endings all over their body. These help them easily find their way in the dark.

A rabbit has sharp **incisors**. The more it nibbles, the more they shrink. Luckily, a rabbit's incisors are always growing—just like your nails.

Rabbits have a phenomenal **nose**, with which they smell everything. They can easily distinguish between what's food and what's not. They can sniff out their friends and their enemies. They can even smell you from the opposite end of the forest!

Rabbits have a good sense of **taste** too. They prefer sweets.

The rabbit family

Though the rabbit and hare are related, they're quite different from each other. Take a look.

A hare is bigger and stronger than a rabbit. Hares have small black spots on the tips of their ears. Their eyes are lighter, and their ears are longer. A hare also has a longer snout and bigger paws.

Hares prefer to live alone, while rabbits live in groups. Hares like open spaces, like a meadow. Rabbits prefer the woods or the dunes. They like having shelter, like shrubberies, or a hill in which they can make a hole. Hares don't dig holes. Instead, they dig a place in the grass (a form).

Did you know a hare can run almost twice as fast as a rabbit?

Here you see some **other family members** of the rabbit.

The marsh rabbit lives in the swamp. It has short ears and likes swimming. When it dives underwater, it holds its breath. Marsh rabbits love water plants.

The pika, or whistling hare, looks like a small mouse. And yet, it's related to the rabbit! It has small, round ears and no tail.

The arctic hare is well equipped to withstand the cold. Since its fur is white, it can easily hide in the snow.

The brush rabbit enjoys high temperatures. It lives in dry and hot surroundings. It has big, long ears to cool down.

What does a rabbit say?

Have you ever spoken to a rabbit? They speak a different language than we do. Would you like to know what they're saying?

I like you.
Rabbits give each other kisses when they like each other. They like cuddling too. If a rabbit licks you, it most definitely likes you.

I'm scared.
If a rabbit opens its eyes widely and grinds its teeth loudly, it's scared or in pain. When a rabbit is very scared, it tucks its ears backwards and screams.

Hello! Who are you?
Rabbits bump into each other with their snouts. That means hello. Then they start sniffing. They recognize each other by their scents. "Who are you? Sniff, sniff . . . Hey, how are you? Nice to smell you!"

This is mine!
A rabbit leaves its scent wherever it goes. It does this through droppings and pee. It also rubs its chin against objects. It's telling other rabbits: "This is mine! I was here first!"

Beware! Danger!
When there's danger, a rabbit stomps its hind legs to alert its friends. Sometimes, it even stomps when it's feeling disagreeable.

I don't like this!
When a rabbit whistles or blows, it's unhappy. When it growls and grumbles, it's angry.

What does a rabbit like?

A rabbit likes peace and quiet. It doesn't like noise.
That's why it's important to set its hutch in a quiet location.
A rabbit likes cuddles and hugs.
Rabbits don't like to be alone. It's best to keep two of them, so they can become friends.
Do you have only one rabbit? Then you have to take it out of the hutch regularly and play with it. You can also set a toy or a stuffed animal in its hutch.

Did you know a rabbit grinds its teeth softly when it's feeling at ease? Sometimes, it makes clicking sounds with its teeth when it's happy.

What does a rabbit eat?

A rabbit loves **fresh food**. But it must be washed. Also, be aware that rabbits can't distinguish between poisonous and non-poisonous foods.

Always make sure there's **water** in its water bottle. Even if the water hasn't run out, you should still change it.

Don't give the rabbit **too much kibble**. One or two tablespoons per rabbit per day is sufficient. Kibble fills its stomach quickly and then the rabbit won't eat other healthy foods. Preferably give it food with only pressed kibble. This contains everything it needs.

A rabbit must eat and drink twice a day.

Munchies are good for its teeth. You can buy special rabbit munchies in the pet store. But you can give it young branches and twigs as well. It also likes stale bread.

Hay is very important to a rabbit. It helps the rabbit to digest its food properly. That's why you must always set enough hay in its hutch. It can never eat too much.

Did you know
rabbits eat their own droppings at night? They're very healthy for them.

Baby rabbits

If you want to have baby rabbits, you need a male (a buck) and a female (a doe). The young ones take about one month to grow in their mother's belly. Usually, there are three to eight of them. Before she gives birth, the mother makes a comfortable nest with straw and hair from her coat. Baby rabbits are blind and bald at birth. Their mother feeds them milk. Within a week, they get a fur of down and then their eyes open. After three weeks, they occasionally leave the nest and begin eating food. After six or seven weeks, they're old enough to leave their mother.

Beware! If possible, don't touch the babies! Soon, your scent will pass to them, and this will upset their mother. If you must touch them, pet the mother first. That way, the babies will keep smelling like their mother.

Wild rabbits

Wild rabbits live in a hole in the woods or in the dunes. You can't pick them up. A wild rabbit is afraid of people. If you touch it, it'll run away quickly.

Rabbits must watch out for foxes, weasels, ermines, pine martens, stone martens, and polecats. They must also watch out for birds of prey, owls, and herring gulls.

Did you know
cats are able to catch a small rabbit?

Tame rabbits

Tame rabbits love people. Some of them live inside a house. Others live in a hutch outside or in a barn. Set a layer of wood shavings and straw in the hutch. And make sure there's a drinking bottle and a bowl for food. Clean the hutch every week, otherwise the rabbit may get sick.

There are many kinds of hutches. Most hutches are actually too small. A rabbit needs space to move and run around.

If you set a **rabbit cage** inside, choose a cool location. Not a place that's sunny, drafty, or close to a heater. Not all rabbits like living inside. Pygmy rabbits, for example, are better equipped for it than a Flemish Giant rabbit.

This hutch is actually too small. So, you must let the rabbit out regularly to run free. Only do this when you're near! Many houseplants are poisonous to rabbits. Also, rabbits like to gnaw on cords and cables, which can be very dangerous.

In a **run**, the rabbit has a lot of space to move around, play, and eat grass. Be sure to set gauze underneath, otherwise the rabbit could start digging and escape. A hutch for the night is also important. A rabbit likes to retreat in a small, dark hole.

Rabbit hill

Rabbits like rabbit hills best. It's like a playground with tubes and tree stumps. Inside the hill, rabbits can dig out their own little hole. There must also be gauze under a rabbit hill, otherwise they'll dig out a tunnel to escape.

Did you know some rabbits live in a rabbit apartment?

In the wild, rabbits like to eat grass, leaves, young branches, and bark. They also eat fruits, berries, and mushrooms.

After three weeks, the young rabbits go outside for the first time.

The Dutch rabbit has a colored backside. Its ears and cheeks are also colored. They're sweet rabbits and are easy to hold.

The Rex rabbit has a beautiful shorthaired, thick velvety coat.

The Belgian hare looks like a hare, but it's actually a rabbit. It has a beautiful slender body.

Rabbit breeds
There are more than 125 kinds of tame rabbits.

Flemish Giant rabbits are the largest rabbits in the world. Some of them are taller than three feet long.

The bearded rabbit from Ghent has long hair around its head and on the sides of its body. It looks like it has a beard.

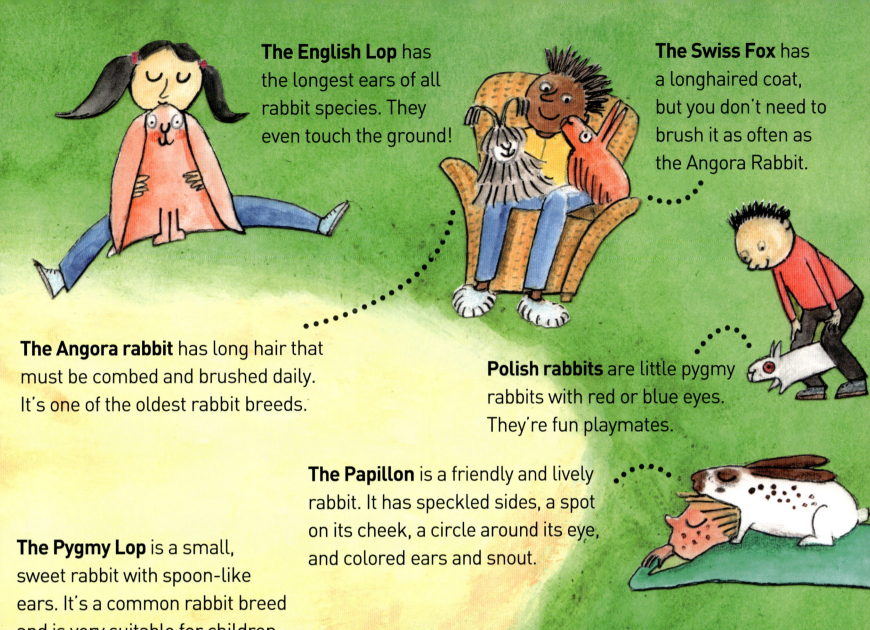

The English Lop has the longest ears of all rabbit species. They even touch the ground!

The Swiss Fox has a longhaired coat, but you don't need to brush it as often as the Angora Rabbit.

The Angora rabbit has long hair that must be combed and brushed daily. It's one of the oldest rabbit breeds.

Polish rabbits are little pygmy rabbits with red or blue eyes. They're fun playmates.

The Papillon is a friendly and lively rabbit. It has speckled sides, a spot on its cheek, a circle around its eye, and colored ears and snout.

The Pygmy Lop is a small, sweet rabbit with spoon-like ears. It's a common rabbit breed and is very suitable for children.

The Big Lorraine is related to the Flemish Giant rabbit. It's also very big! It has a line on its back and five to eight spots on its sides.

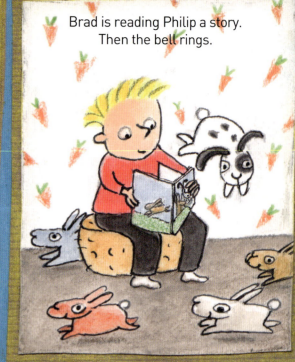

Brad catches the rabbits and brings them inside, one after another.

Philip is gone! I can't find him anywhere!

Look who's popping up out of the hat!

Sweet Little Rabbit

(To the melody of: *Are You Sleeping* [*Brother John*]?)

My sweet rabbit, my sweet rabbit.
Come over here.
Come over here.
I would like a warm hug.
I would like a warm hug.
I beg you, please.
I beg you, please.

My soft rabbit, my soft rabbit.
Come over here.
Come over here.
I would like a sweet hug.
I would like a sweet hug.
I beg you, please.
I beg you, please.

I'm Building a Hutch

Tap, tap, tap.
I'm building a hutch.
I'm building a hutch for my rabbit.
I'll even build a fountain.

Hammer, hammer, saw.
I'm building a room.
I'm building a room for my rabbit.
I'll paint the walls with flowers.

Hammer, hammer, drill.
I'm building a house.
I'm building a house for my rabbit.
The curtains are made of silk.